The Blackfeet Nation

by Allison Lassieur

Consultant:
Chief Earl Old Person
Blackfeet Nation of Montana

Bridgestone Books
an imprint of Capstone Press
Mankato, Minnesota

Bridgestone Books are published by Capstone Press
151 Good Counsel Drive, P.O. Box 669, Mankato, Minnesota 56002
http://www.capstone-press.com

Library of Congress Cataloging-in-Publication Data
Lassieur, Allison.
    The Blackfeet nation/by Allison Lassieur.
    p. cm.—(Native peoples)
    Includes bibliographical references and index.
    ISBN 0-7368-0946-5
    1. Siksika Indians—History—Juvenile literature. 2. Siksika Indians—Social life and customs—Juvenile literature. 3. Sihasapa Indians—History—Juvenile literature. 4. Sihasapa Indians—Social life and customs—Juvenile literature. [1. Siksika Indians. 2. Indians of North America.] I. Title. II. Series.
E99.S54 L35 2002
971.23′004973—dc21   00-013127

Summary: An overview of the past and present of the Blackfeet Nation, including a
    description of their homes, food, clothing, religion, family life, and government.

Editorial Credits
Rebecca Glaser, editor; Karen Risch, product planning editor; Timothy Halldin, cover
    designer; Heidi Meyer, illustrator; Jeff Anderson, photo researcher

Photo Credits
Alan G. Nelson/Root Resources, 14
Dan Polin, cover
D & L Photography, 12
Kit Breen, 8, 10
Marilyn "Angel" Wynn, 16, 18
National Museum of the American Indian, 6, 20

1 2 3 4 5 6 07 06 05 04 03 02

Table of Contents

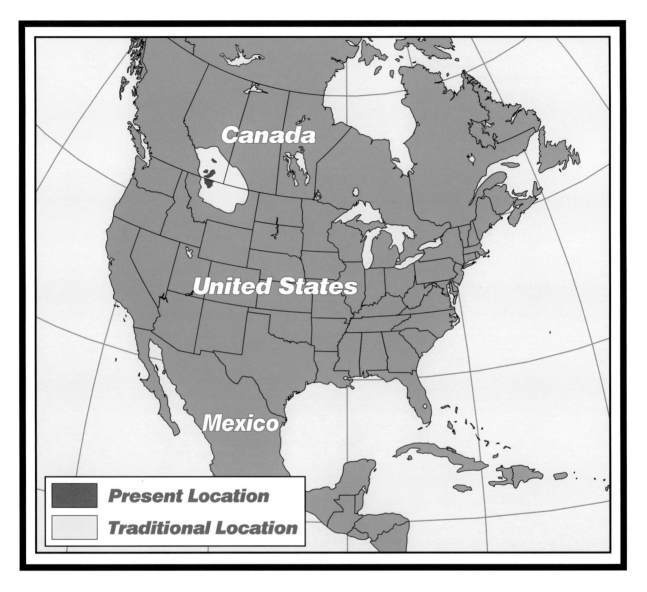

Present Location

Traditional Location

Blackfeet tribes once lived in the northwestern Great Plains. Their land stretched from the Saskatchewan River in Canada to the Missouri River in Montana. Today, the Blackfeet live on reservations in Montana and in Alberta, Canada.

Fast Facts

The Blackfeet tribe once hunted buffalo on the northern Great Plains. Today, there are four tribes of Blackfeet. One tribe lives in Montana. The other three tribes live in the Canadian province of Alberta. The tribes share a common history. The Blackfeet are proud of their past.

Homes: The Blackfeet lived in large tepees. These cone-shaped homes were made of long poles and buffalo hides. Tepees were easy to take apart and move from place to place.

Food: Blackfeet tribes ate buffalo for most of their food. They also hunted and ate elk, deer, and other animals. Women gathered berries and other wild plants.

Clothing: The Blackfeet made clothing out of animal skins. Women wore long dresses made from soft skins. Men dressed in leggings, shirts, breechcloths, and moccasins. In winter, people wrapped themselves in buffalo skin robes to keep warm.

Language: The Blackfeet language is part of the Algonquian language family. Native Americans in eastern North America spoke Algonquian languages. The Blackfeet were one of the few Great Plains tribes that spoke a language from this family.

In 1874, some Blackfeet moved to a reservation in Montana.

Blackfeet History

The Blackfeet hunted buffalo on the northwestern plains of North America. They traded with other tribes for horses and guns. The Blackfeet became very powerful.

In the 1850s, white settlers began moving onto Blackfeet land. The U.S. government signed treaties with the Blackfeet. These agreements gave Blackfeet hunting land to the United States. The U.S. government would pay for the land with food and supplies. But the U.S. government did not keep its part of the agreement. In 1874, the government moved one group of Blackfeet to a reservation in Montana. Three years later, three groups of Blackfeet moved to reserves in Canada.

By 1884, white settlers had killed almost all of the buffalo. Many Blackfeet starved. For many years, the Blackfeet depended on the U.S. government for survival. Today, the Blackfeet have their own government and take care of their own people.

The Blackfeet People

No one is sure how the Blackfeet received their name. One legend says black soot from a prairie fire turned the people's shoes black. Some people think that the Blackfeet painted their moccasins black. Another name for the Blackfeet was "Lords of the Plains." The Blackfeet tribe was one of the most powerful tribes on the Great Plains.

Today, the Blackfeet are divided into four tribes. The Pikuni/Piegan live on a reservation in Montana. The North Piegan Pikuni, the Blood/Kainai, and the Blackfoot/Siksika live on reserves in Alberta, Canada. Together these tribes are known as the Blackfeet Confederacy. The tribes have separate governments, but they come together for religious celebrations.

Every summer, Blackfeet from all four tribes gather in Montana for North American Indian Days. They celebrate this event with ceremonies, dances, games, and parades.

The Blackfeet hold a parade during North American Indian Days.

Homes, Food, and Clothing

The Blackfeet lived in large tepees. Blackfeet women built these cone-shaped homes by covering long poles with many buffalo skins. The Blackfeet painted designs on their tepees.

Most of the Blackfeet's food came from buffalo. They boiled, roasted, or dried the buffalo meat. Blackfeet men also hunted elk, deer, moose, and mountain sheep. Women gathered berries and other wild plants. People ate pemmican during winter. Pemmican was a mixture of ground buffalo meat, berries, and buffalo fat.

The Blackfeet made most of their clothing from animal skins. Women made antelope or mountain sheep skins into long dresses that had straps. In the winter, women sewed long sleeves onto the dresses. Men wore leggings, shirts, breechcloths, and moccasins. Everyone dressed in warm buffalo robes in the winter. The Blackfeet decorated clothing with fringe, porcupine quills, and painted designs.

This modern tepee shows traditional Blackfeet designs.

The Blackfeet Family

Blackfeet parents once arranged marriages for their children. The man had to prove to the bride's father that he was a powerful warrior and a good hunter. The marriage was complete when the man and woman gave each other gifts such as horses and clothing. The couple then lived with the man's family or in their own tepee.

Blackfeet parents taught their children Blackfeet ways of life. Mothers taught girls how to cook and how to prepare buffalo hides. Girls played with dolls stuffed with buffalo hair. Fathers taught boys how to hunt. Boys played with toy bows and arrows. Both girls and boys learned how to ride horses at an early age.

Today, family still is important to the Blackfeet. Many families live together on the reservations. Mothers, fathers, and grandparents help raise children and teach them the Blackfeet language.

Family is important to the Blackfeet.

Napi and the First People

The Blackfeet have many stories about the Old Man, or Napi. The Blackfeet call these stories "Napi stories." They believe that Napi is the creator of the universe. This story tells how Napi taught the first people to survive.

Napi showed the first people the plants that he had made. He showed them roots and berries and said, "You can eat these." He pointed to certain trees and said, "When the bark of these trees is young and tender, peel it off and eat it." He taught them how to use other plants to heal sickness.

Napi pointed to the animals in the world. "You can eat the animals," he said. He showed the people how to make bows and arrows out of wood. Napi taught them how to shoot animals and birds. He then showed the first people how to make fire and cook food. The first people listened to Napi and learned how to live in the world.

Napi taught the Blackfeet how to use animals, plants, and trees to survive in the world.

Blackfeet Religion

Years ago, the Blackfeet believed that everything in the world had special power. A Blackfeet man sometimes received the power of an animal or a place in a dream. The animal or the place would give the dreamer a list of stories, songs, and objects. The dreamer had to gather all of the objects and put them in a special medicine bundle. He used the stories, songs, and medicine bundle to call the power.

Today, some Blackfeet still practice traditional religion. The Blackfeet still use medicine bundles. Five tribal members are bundle holders. They care for the Blackfeet's five special medicine bundles. The five bundle holders have a ceremony at the first sound of thunder in the spring. They open one bundle. The next time it thunders, they hold another ceremony. They continue to hold ceremonies until all the bundles are opened. In this way, the Blackfeet welcome spring to the land.

Medicine bundles are important in the Blackfeet religion.

The Eagle Staff

The Blackfeet Eagle Staff is an important object to the tribe. The Eagle Staff is a tall stick decorated with colorful designs and feathers. The chief uses it at ceremonies and gatherings. The Eagle Staff is a symbol of pride and power to the Blackfeet.

The Eagle Staff is similar to a great battle coup (KOO) stick. A coup was an act of great bravery to the Blackfeet. A Blackfeet warrior touched an enemy during battle but did not kill him. A coup showed bravery because being close to the enemy was dangerous. A warrior's battle coup stick was decorated with designs that told of the warrior's victories in battle.

Years ago, only certain Blackfeet warriors were allowed to have coup sticks. These men usually were the leaders of special groups called warrior societies. A warrior society was responsible for protecting the tribe. Members also organized hunting groups and guarded the hunting camps.

The Eagle Staff is a symbol of pride and power to the Blackfeet.

Blackfeet Government

Years ago, the Blackfeet did not live together in one tribe. They were separated into bands. Each band had a war chief and a civil chief. The war chief was chosen because of his bravery in battle. The civil chief was a person who could speak well and lead people in times of peace.

Today, each Blackfeet reservation has its own government. They each have a tribal council. Some reservations have a chairperson of the council. Other tribes call this leader the head chief.

The Blackfeet in Montana have a council with eight members and one chairperson. Each member of the council is elected by the Blackfeet people. The Montana Blackfeet also have a tribal chief. His name is Chief Earl Old Person. He will be tribal chief for the rest of his life.

Two Guns White Calf was a leader of the Piegan Blackfeet in the late 1800s. He led the tribe until he died on a trip to Washington, D.C., in 1903.

Hands On: Learn Blackfeet Words

The Blackfeet language is important to the tribe. Members want to preserve their culture and language. Children learn how to speak Blackfeet in school.

Bread	Na'pay'innah-pie-in
Cereal	Ksi-ska-noh-sin
Crackers	Mi-ksi-kaa-pa-yin
Macaroni	Aissiniip
Rice	Aiskssinainakin
Cup	Kos
Fork	Ih-toh-yiop
Knife	Ist-toh-waan
Napkin	Ih-tais-so'yiop
Today	Aa-nohk-ksi-tsi-tsi-koi
Tomorrow	Ai-pi-na-ko's
Yesterday	Maa-toon-ni
Bus Driver	Isski-nii-matai-ksi
Cook	Ooyosi
Doctor	Aisokinaki
Nurse	Aisokinakiaakii
Police Officer	Iyinnakiikoowon

Words to Know

breechcloth (BREECH-kloth)—a piece of deerskin clothing that hangs from the waist and passes between the legs
ceremony (SER-eh-moh-nee)—formal actions, words, and music that honor a person, an event, or a higher being
confederacy (kuhn-FED-ur-uh-see)—a union of towns or tribes with a common goal
coup (KOO)—an act of great bravery; a Blackfeet warrior touched an enemy during battle, but did not kill him.
religion (ri-LIJ-uhn)—a set of spiritual beliefs people follow
reservation (rez-er-VAY-shun)—land owned and controlled by American Indians
tepee (TEE-pee)—a cone-shaped tent made of animal skins
tradition (truh-DISH-uhn)—a custom, idea, or belief that is passed on to younger people by older relatives
treaty (TREE-tee)—a formal agreement between two or more governments or nations

Read More

Kavasch, E. Barrie. *Blackfoot Children and Elders Talk Together.* Library of Intergenerational Learning. Native Americans. New York: PowerKids Press, 1999.
Press, Petra. *The Blackfeet.* First Reports. Minneapolis: Compass Point Books, 2001.

Useful Addresses

Blackfeet Nation
P.O. Box 850
Browning, MT 59417

Blood Tribe
P.O. Box 60
Stand Off, AB T0L 1Y0
Canada

Piegan Nation
P.O. Box 70
Brocket, AB T0K 0N0
Canada

Siksika Nation
P.O. Box 1100
Siksika, AB T0J 3W0
Canada

Internet Sites

Blackfeet Community College
http://www.montana.edu/wwwbcc
The Blackfeet Nation
http://www.blackfeetnation.com
The Blackfeet Today
http://www.lewis-clark.org/black_today.htm

Index